I0017974

Table of Contents

Introduction

Getting started in coding can be tough. You may have looked at a few of the most popular coding languages, such as C++ or Java and been a bit scared by what you saw. The pages may have been filled to the brim with letters and symbols that you just didn't understand, and you became frustrated and just wanted to walk away. Many people are scared of programing and feel like it is just too hard for them. But with the Python programming language, you will find that it can be easier than ever to learn about coding and to even read it like a professional.

This guidebook is going to give you some of the basics that you need to get started with Python programming. We will start out a bit talking about what Python programming is as well as some of the steps that you should take in order to download the program, if it isn't already present on your computer, and give you some more information to really understand why this program is so great. We will then move on to some keywords that will be useful to you when starting out with the program and even talk about the benefits and the drawbacks of using Python for all your coding and programing needs.

The rest of the guidebook is devoted to talking about some of the different things that you can do within the Python program as well as some examples of how each of these would work. We talk about adding comments into the code, working with strings and integers, and even spend some time working with variables so that they will show up right in the program. It is a great idea to experiment a bit with the process. Python makes it easy to test out your strings so that you can figure out what is going to work and what needs some more practice.

Getting started in programing can seem like a challenge. You may worry that you aren't going to be able to figure it all out and all of those crazy programing languages may have scared you away in the first place. This guidebook is going to spend some time looking at the Python language and exploring how easy it can be to get started with this simple program.

Chapter 1: Learning About Python

The computer world has brought in many different types of people. Some are interested in making money creating their own programs to sell to others. Some just like to mess around and learn different things about how the computer will work. And still others have devoted their lives to programming, making it the product that brings home their income each month whether they work at repairing computers, work in a corporation to keep the computers safe, or doing some other aspect of computer technology.

When it comes to computer technology, nothing is going to be simple. Before you can even get a program to work on the computer, it needs to receive the right code to make it work. There are several options for code creation that a computer tech can choose including Java, C++ and Python. Here we will explore a bit about Python and why it is often preferred over the other two programming options.

Before you are able to start using Python to take over your programming needs, it is important to start learning more about it and all of the great benefits you will receive when using this program. Python is a high level programming tool, which means that it is easy to use and read, even as a beginner. The philosophy behind the code is readability and it has a type of syntax that allows the programmer to express their concepts without having pages of code along with it. Compared to using other popular codes, like Java and C++, this can make Python much easier to complete.

The philosophy of this code language is simple enough to use. It believes that a simple design is so much better than a complex one and that readability is important. This is a great language for beginners to get started on because they will actually be able to read and understand the code they are putting in. With other options, they may have to spend a lot of time trying to get the code just right, adding in many other symbols to get it to work. But with Python, it is kept much simpler and you may find that it is easier to read through the lines and see what you are doing.

Some of the features that you may like with Python include:

- An elegant syntax which will make the programs so easy to read.

- Language that is easy to use so that the program will work without a lot of bugs. If you are doing ad hoc programming tasks or prototype development because it works well without issues with maintaining the program.

- Has a large library that will work with other programming tasks such as changing files, searching for text, and connecting with web servers.

- Python is really interactive. This makes it easier for you to test out small bits of code to see if they work. You can also bundle it with a development environment called IDLE.

- If you would like to expand the programming language, it is easy to extend into other modules like C or C++.

- Python programming can be run on any unit including Unix, Linux, Windows, and Mac OS X.

- The software is free. You won't have to pay anything to download and use Python in your own life. you can also make modifications and redistribute this product. It is under a license, but it is an open source license so others are able to use it.

- Even though Python is a simple programming language, it does contain some advanced features like list comprehensions and generators.

- Errors can be caught quickly in this programming. Since data types are dynamically typed, when you mix types together that don't match, it will raise an exception for you to notice.

- You can group the codes into packages and modules if needed.
- There is a wide variety of basic data types that you can choose from including dictionaries, lists, strings, and numbers.

The Origins of Python

The beginning of the modern Python programming started in December of 1989. The creator of this program was Guido van Rossum who began programming as more of a hobby. At the time, van Rossum was working on a project with the Dutch CWI research institute, that was later terminated. Van Rossum was able to use some of the basics of this new language, known as the ABC language, in order to work on Python.

The main strength of this language is that it is really easy to extend upon to make more complex, or keep simple, and it was able to support multiple platforms. Both of these were important during the days when personal computers were becoming popular. And since Python was designed to communicate with different file formats and libraries, it became a hit as well.

Python has grown quite a bit since its inception and more tools have been added to make the programing more functioning. In addition to making Python easy to use, van Rossum has been working on initiatives that encourage the education of coding to everyone, not just a select few. Using Python to use coding can make things easier and helps to get rid of some of the fears associated with the complex computer codes since it doesn't look so scary.

Over the years, van Rossum decided to make Python open sourced. This allowed all to gain access and make changes to Python so that if something happened to van Rossum, all would not be lost. Thanks to having Python open sourced, Python 2.0 was released during 2000 to make it more community oriented and to have a transparent development process. There are a few newer versions of Python 2.0 still being used, but Python 3 has been taking the world by storm and most anticipate this will be the normal one used within the next few years.

Python 3

This version of Python was released in 2008. It is not simply an update to the program, but a complete change in it. While there are a lot of great features that come with this version, it doesn't have a backward compatibility so you will have to make a choice between Python 2.0 and Python 3. To make things easier, the programmers did make a little marker within the program that would show a coder what needed to be changed between the two programs when uploading. Despite this, most have stuck with Python 2.0 for now.

Why Use Python?

As you can probably guess, there are several different computer coding programs that you can choose to use. But while there are some benefits to using these other programs, Python is one of the best options out there. It is easy to use, has a lot of options for you to choose from, and it can even be used over a variety of platforms without having to change things up. Some of the benefits that you will love with Python include:

Readability

Python is designed to work with the English language, making it easy to read. There are also strict rules in terms of punctuation on the program so you aren't just looking at brackets all over the place. Python also makes sure that the programmer knows how to format everything thanks to a set of rules that are in place, making it easy for everyone to create a code that others can follow.

Libraries

Python has been around for over 25 years now and since it is one of the easiest codes to learn how to use, there have been quite a few different codes written using the system. The good news is that this system is open sourced so that the code is available for any programmer to use. You can install the Python program in your own system and use it for your own personal use. Whether you are using the codes to finish off a product or to write some of your own codes, the library of Python is easy to use. The codes that you want will be installed into the libraries and since the program has been around for a long tie, they are going to cover pretty much whatever you want from automating your server to making changes to a picture.

Community

Since Python is so popular, the community for Python is pretty big. There are conferences with lots of networking and workshops available for this programming products and lots of places you can visit, both online and offline, to ask questions or to learn more about the program. You may want to consider checking out a few of these places if you are a beginner with Python as it can help you to learn more and even to meet some new people.

If you are interested in getting started with coding, Python is one of the best options that you can make. It is simple to get started on and since it will work on a variety of different platforms, it is sure to work on your personal computer. Since it is easy to read, you will find that coding doesn't have to be a challenge and you can create your own, or learn from others in no time.

Chapter 2: The Benefits and Negatives of Python

Python is a great program to use whether you are a beginner in the programming world or you have been into it for some time. Many of those who are just looking at getting started with programming will jump right in with Python and make it their own. It is simple to understand and can be used by anyone who is ready to get started with coding. This chapter is going to take some time to explain some of the positives, as well as some of the drawbacks, of using Python for your programming language.

The Benefits of Python

Python is probably one of the best programming languages that you can choose to use. Beginners are going to love how easy it is to turn on this program and start writing their own codes, even without experience, and there is plenty to enjoy when you are a professional, or an expert, as well. Some of the benefits that you will get when you get started with Python include:

Easy to use and read

When it comes to programming language, there are none that are as easy to use as Python. Other languages are kind of clunky and hard to look at. You may take a look at them and notice that they have tons of brackets and even words that you won't even recognize. It is enough to scare away someone who isn't used to programming at all just because all the words look a bit intimidating.

Python is a bit different. Instead of all the crazy brackets, it makes use of indentations, causing an easier to read page that isn't such a mess. Instead of words that you can't understand, it uses English. The other special characters are kept to a minimum so that you can look at the page of code and not feel like you are going to be overwhelmed in the process.

This is one of the easiest programming tools that you can use. It looks nice on the page and will use plenty of white spaces, when it can, to make it easier to read what you should know. There are also plenty of places with comments so you can get clarification if a program is too confusing for you. Overall, it is one of the best programming languages to use to really get ahead or even to learn about programming.

Uses English as the main language

Since English is the language that this program is based off, it is really easy to read. There aren't a lot of words that you won't get and you won't have to spend time trying to figure out what it is telling you. The program is all in English and you will love how simple this can make things.

Already present on some computers

In some cases, Python is already present on your computer. Mac OS X systems as well as those with Ubuntu will already have Python preloaded. You will simply need to download a text interpreter to get started. In terms of using Python on Windows computers, all you need to do is download the program. Python works with all of these programs, even if it isn't installed right from the beginning.

Can work with other programming languages

In the beginning, you will most likely only use Python on its own. It is a great program to learn with and grow with. But over time, you may decide that you want to try something new that Python can't do on its own. Luckily, Python is able to work with several other programming languages, such as C++ and JavaScript, so you can mess around, learn some more, and really get the code that you are looking for, even if Python is not able to do all the work.

Can test out things with the interpreter

When you download Python, you are going to have to download a text interpreter too. This will make it easier for Python to read through your information. You can use simple products that are sometimes already on your computer, such as Notepad from Windows or look for another interpreter that may be a bit easier.

Once you pick out the interpreter that you would like to use, it is time to get to work writing the code. Some of those who are new to coding may feel worried about trying to get the code to work. This is another spot where Python can make things easier. It will be able to take the words that you are typing and spit them back out, with the help of the interpreter, in just a few seconds. You can test what you are doing while you are working on it!

There are so many benefits of using the Python program. Beginners are going to love how readily available this program is and how easy it is to learn some of the simple commands in no time. Even those who have been programming for some time will be impressed by how this all works!

The Negatives of Python

While there are a lot of reasons to love Python, it is important to realize that there are a few negatives that you should watch out for. These negatives include:

It doesn't have a lot of speed

For those who are looking to work with a program that has a lot of speed, Python may not always be the best option for you. It is an interpreted language so this will slow it down compared to some of the other options that are compiled languages. However, it does depend on what you are translating.

There are certain benchmarks with the Python code that can run faster using PyPy compared to other codes.

Luckily this issue with a slow speed and Python is being remedied. Programmers are working to make the interpreting speed of Python faster so that you won't have to compare it with the others so much. Over time, the hope is that Python will be able to work at the same speed as C and C++ or even some of the newer programming languages that are coming out.

Not present on most mobile browsers

Python is a great option to use if you have a regular computer. It is available on many desktop and server platforms to help you create the code that you are looking for. But it is not ready to go into mobile computing. Since there is such a big increase in revenue and people going into the mobile industry, it is sad that this programming language hasn't kept up with the trends like others.

Perhaps in the future Python will decide to go into the future and develop a version that will be able to work well with various mobile devices. Until then, programmers will have to be satisfied with using it on their desktop and laptop computers.

Restrictions with the design

If you are looking to work with a program that has a lot of design options, the Python program may not be the right option for you. The design language is not up to what you will find with some of the other option. Since you are working with a program that is dynamically typed, it takes more testing and can have more errors that will only show up when you are running the program.

The global interpreter lock means that you can only have one thread access the internals of Python at a time. This may not be as important anymore since it is easy to spawn the tasks out to different processes, but the design is not as nice as some of the other options that you would like.

A good way to work with the design is to remember that indentation is important with Python. Other programming languages are going to use a lot of brackets to show the difference in lines and information inside the program, but Python is going to rely on indentations. Make sure to be careful with using this to avoid issues and errors that can come up.

Python can be one of the best programs that you use to write your own codes and have some fun. While there are a lot of benefits to using this program, especially compared to some of the other ones that aren't as easy to read, it is important to understand both the positives and negatives of each option before you jump in!

Chapter 3: Common Terms You Should Know with Python

Before you get too far into your programming with Python, it is important to understand some of the words that can make the programming easier to understand. This chapter is going to take some time to look at the different words that are common in Python programming, and which we do talk about a bit in this guidebook, to help avoid some confusion and to help you get started with your first code.

- Class—this is a template that was used for creating user-defined objects.
- Docstring—this is a string that will appear lexically first expression inside a module, function, or class definition. The object will be available to documentation tools.
- Function—this is a block of code that is invoked when using a calling program. It is best used in order to provide a calculation or an

autonomous service.

- IDLE—this stands for Integrated Development Environment for Python. This is the basic interpreter and editor environment that you can use along with Python. It is good for those who are just beginning with this and can work for those on a budget. It is a clear example of code and won't waste a lot of time or space.

- Immutable—this is an object within the code that is assigned a fixed value. This could include tuples, strings, and numbers. You can't alter the object and you will need to create a new object with a different value and store it first. This can be helpful in some cases, such as the keys in a dictionary.

- Interactive—one thing that a lot of beginners like about Python is that it is so interactive. You can try out some different things in the interpreter and see how they will react right away in the results. It is a good way to improve your programming skills, test out a new idea you have and more.

- List—this is a datatype within Python that is built in. It contains a mutable sequence of values that are sorted. It can include immutable values of numbers and strings as well.

- Mutable—these are the objects that will be able to change their value within the program, but which are able to keep their original id().

- Object—within Python, this is any data with a state, such as a value or an attribute, as well as a defined behavior, or a method.

- Python 3000—Python 2 and Python 3 are the main two types of Python that are available. Many people have stuck with Python 2 since Python 3 does not have any backwards capabilities and they like using the databases on the older version. Python 3000 is a mythical option of Python that does allow this backward capability so you can use it and the Python 2.

- String—this is one of the most basic types that you will find in Python that will store the text. In Python 2, the strings will store text so that the string type can then be used to hold onto binary data.

- Triple quoted string—this is a string that has three instances of either the single quote or the double quote. It could have something like '"I love tacos"'. They are used for many reasons. They can help you to have double and single quotes in a string and they make it easier to go over a few lines of code without issues.

- Tuple—this is a datatype that has been built into Python. This datatype is an immutable ordered sequence of values. The sequence is the only part that is immutable. It can contain some mutable values, such as having a dictionary inside it, where the value's can change.

- Type—this is a category or sort of data that is represented in the programming languages. These types are going to differ in their properties, they including immutable and mutable options, as well as in their functions and methods. Python includes a few of these including dictionary types, tuple, list, floating point, long, integer, and string.

•

Chapter 4: Getting Started with Python

Now that we know some of the benefits of choosing this program, it is time to get started with it. Before you are able to learn some of the great steps that are needed to make this program create code for you, it is time to set up the environment. For those who have a computer with Mac OS X or Ubuntu, you will already have Python installed on the system This can make things easier to get started as you will just need to click on the icon to get started.

Windows computers will need to install Python. While Python works just fine on Windows computers, it doesn't come preinstalled so you will need to do this. The following steps work for Windows 7 to 10:

- Download Python—you can choose between Python 2 or Python 3. Both are fantastic options; it just depends on which one will get the job done for you.

- Click to run the Python Installer. When you get to the options, choose to Customize Installation.
- You will see a box pop up. Click on every box that is under Optional Features and then continue.
- On the next screen, look for the Advanced Options and then choose where you would like to have Python install.

Once you have gotten this far, the next part is to set up your PATH variable. This is going to allow the user to include directories for all the components and packages that are needed. To do this step:

- Open up the Control Panel on the Windows computer.
- Look up Environment.
- Under System Environment Variable, click on Edit. Then click on Environment Variables.
- You may have to look a bit for the next part, but look for User Variables. You can then either create a new one or edit an existing path.
  - To create a new path, select PATH as the name and add it to the directories that are there. Make sure that each Variable Values is separated with a semicolon.
  - If you want to edit your existing path, you need to make sure that each value is on a different line. Click on New and then put your

directories on different lines.

- Now you can open your command prompt. To do this click on Start then Windows System and then Command Prompt.
- When the command prompt opens, you can type in "Python." This will load up the Python interpreter. You can then type in Exit and hit Enter to get back to the command prompt.

Text Editor

You will not be able to program Python without having the text editor in place on your computer. If you are using Windows, the Notepad function will work. Make sure that you are not using Word though, it is not considered an editor and your code is not going to save on the system properly. If you are considering getting a version of Notepad, you will notice that Notepad ++ is the best one to use on a Windows computer and Text Wrangler is the best to use for Mac. To set them up, do the following:

Windows

Download and then install Notepad ++

Once it is downloaded, open up the settings and click on Language Menu and

Tab Settings

Tick the box that is beside Expand Tabs

Make sure that the value is at 4.

Click again to Close.

Mac

Download and then install Text Wrangler

You won't need to register to install the software, just click Cancel if there is a box that comes up asking for this.

Otherwise, follow the other instructions that come on the screen to set this editor up.

Once the program is on your computer it is time to learn more about the coding and functions that you can enjoy on Python.

Getting IDLE

While you are setting up Python, make sure that you download the IDLE or the

Integrated Development and Learning Environment. This should download along with Python if you are setting it up, but make sure to check into this while you are going through the process. This is the environment that you are going to work with when you are on Python and it can make things easy. If you don't want to mess around with finding another environment or you want to make the process as easy as possible for you as a beginner, this is the option for you.

The main features of using IDLE with your Python programming include:

- Integrated debugger with persistent breakpoints, call stack visibility, and stepping to make things easier
- Python shell that will highlight the syntax
- Multi-window text editor that can help with the indentation, highlighting, and completing the code.

Now, you can choose to use another environment, like those that we discussed above if needed, but since this one often comes as an option with Python and it is designed to work well with this system, there are many people who choose to go with this option. That being said, there have been some issues in the past with IDLE having trouble focusing, won't copy some things, and some clients don't like the interface design. You may want to try out this program ahead of time and see if it is the right one for you or if you would like to use one of the options above.

Getting Python set up on your computer is a pretty easy process. There are already several types of computers that have the programming language already present so you won't have to do any work and the rest of them simply need a quick download to complete. You can wait just a short amount of time to get Python on your computer and then you are good to go and try out some of the codes you want to make.

Chapter 5: Learning the Basics of Python Programming

Now it is time to get to know a bit more about Python programming and how you can make it work for you. You will need to learn a bit more about the different keywords and the variables that come with Python so you are able to write the words that you want and make the program perform in a certain way. Let's take a look at some of these basics of Python programming so you can get started with your new code right away.

Keywords

When you are working on a new computer coding program, you are going to notice that each computer language will have certain keywords. These are the words that are meant for a specific command or purpose in the language and you should try to avoid using them anywhere else. If you do use these words in other parts of your code, you may end up with an error alert or the program not working properly. The keywords that are reserved for Python include:

- And
- Pass
- Or not
- Nonlocal
- None
- Lambda
- Is
- In import
- If
- Global
- From
- For
- Finally
- False
- Except
- Else
- Elif
- Del
- Def

- Continue

- Class

- Break

- Assert

- As

- Yield

- With

- While

- Try

- True

- Return

- Raise

Identifier Names

When you are creating a new program in Python, you are going to work on creating quite a few entities, a combination of functions, classes, and variables. All o these will be given a name that is also known as an identifier. There are a few rules that you need to follow when forming an identifier in Python including:

- It should contain letters, either uppercase or lowercase or a combination of the two, numbers, and the underscore. You should not see any spaces inside.

- The identifier can't start with a number
- The identifier can't be a keyword and it shouldn't include one of the keywords inside.

If you break one of these rules, the program will close on you and will show a syntax error. In addition, you need to work on making identifiers that are legible to the human eye. While the identifier may make sense to the computer and get through without causing issues on the computer, a human is the one who will read through the code to use it themselves. If the human eye doesn't understand what you are writing in a certain place, you could run into some issues. Some of the rules that you should follow when creating an identifier that will be readable to the human eye include:

- The identifier should be descriptive—you should pick out name that is going to describe what is inside the variable or will describe what it does.
- You should be careful with using abbreviations that aren't necessary because these always make things that are difficult.

While there are a lot of ways that you can write out your code, you should be careful and stick with one rule throughout. For example, both MyBestFriend and mybestfriend work in the coding world, but pick one that you like and do it the same each time that you work in the program to avoid confusion. You can also add in underscores into this or numbers, just be careful that you keep things consistent.

Flow of Control

When working on the Python language, you are going to write out the statements in a list format, just like you would when writing out a shopping list. The computer will start with the first instruction before working through each of them in the order that you make them show up on the list. So you will need to write out the controls that you want just like you would for your grocery shopping list to make sure that the computer is reading it properly. The computer will only stop reading through this list once it has done the final instruction to completion. This is known as the flow of control.

This is an important way to get started. You want to make sure that your flow of control is even and smooth for the computer to read. This will make it easier to get the program to do what you would like without as many issues and ensures that the computer program doesn't get stuck, cause issues, or have something else go wrong.

Semi-colons and Indentation

When you look at some of the other computer languages, you will notice that there are a lot of curly brackets used to arrange the different blocks of code or to begin and end the statements. This helps you to remember to indent the code blocks in these languages to make the code easier to read, although the computer will be able to read the different codes without the indentations just fine.

This type of coding can make it really difficult to read. You will see a lot of unnecessary information that is required for the computer to read the code, but can make it hard on the human eye to read this. Python uses a different way of doing this, mostly to help make it easier on the human eye to read what you have. You are going to need to ident the code for this to work. An example of this is:

 # this function definition begins a new block

def add_numbers (a, b):

c= a + b

as is this one

return c

 # this function definition begins a new block

if it is Saturday

print (It's Tuesday!"

 # and this one is outside the block

print ("Print this no matter what.")

In addition, there are a lot of languages that will use a semicolon to tell when an instruction ends. With Python though, you will use line ends to tell the computer when an instruction will end. You will be able to use a semi-colon if you have a few instructions that are on the same line, but this is often considered bad form within the language.

Letter Case

Most computer languages will treat uppercase and lowercase letters the same, but Python is one of the only ones that will be case sensitive. This means that the lower case and upper case letters will be treated differently in the system. Keep in mind as well that all the reserved words will use lower case except for None, False, and true.

These basics are going to make it easier to get started on the Python programming. You need to take a bit of time to go through the program in order to get familiar with it. You aren't going to need to become an expert, but getting familiar with some of the text interpreter and some of the other parts of the program can make it easier to use and you can learn how the different buttons will work even before you get started. Try out a few of the examples above first to help you get started.

Python works to keep things as basic as possible because it understands that most of its users are going to be beginners or those who are tired of other complex languages. As you can see here, and in the following chapters, there are simple commands that you will be able to put forward in order to get the program to work a specific way. Study these and you can make a great program without quite as much work.

Chapter 6: A Bit More on Comments

There are a lot of things that you can do in Python. It is one of the most interactive options that you will run into when getting started in programming and since it is so easy to use. In this chapter, we will take some time to discuss more about comments and some of the other aspects of Python so you are able to get started and make your codes amazing in no time.

In Python programming a comment is one that will start with the # sign and then will continue on until you get to the end of the line. For example:

 # This would be a comment

print("Hi, how are you?)

This would tell the computer to just print "Hi, how are you?" All comments are ignored in the Python interpreter because it is more of a footnote in the program to help the programmer, or others who may use the code, special things about the code. They are basically there to say what the program is supposed to do and how it will work. It is a bit more detailed and can be helpful without getting in the way of how the code works.

You will not need to leave a comment on every line, just when it is needed. If the programmer feels that something needs explained better, they would put in a comment but don't expect to see it all over the place. Python doesn't support any comments that will go across several lines so if you have a longer comment in the program, figure out how to split it up into different lines with the # sign in front of each part.

Writing and Reading

Some programs are going to show the text you want on the screen, or they can request certain information. You may want to start out the program code by telling the reader what your program is all about. Giving it a name or a title can make things easier so the other coder knows what is in the program and can pick the right one for them.

The best way to get the right information to show up is show a string literal that will include the "print" function. For those who don't know, string literals are basically lines of text that will be surrounded by some quotes, either a single or double quote. The type of quote that you use isn't going to matter that much, but if you use one type in the beginning of the phrase, you should use it at the end. So if there are double quotes at the beginning of your phrase, make sure that you keep up with the double quotes at the end as well.

When you want the computer to display a word or phrase on the screen, you would simply have "print" and then the phrase after it. For example, if you want to portray "Welcome!" you would do

Print("Welcome!")

This will make it so that "Welcome" shows up on your program for others to use. The print function is going to take up its own line so you will notice that after putting this in, the code will automatically place you on a new line.

If you would like to have the visitor do a certain action, you can go with the same kind of idea. For example, say you want the person to input a specific number so that they can get through the code you would use the string:

first_number = input('put the first number in')

When using the input feature, you won't automatically see it print on a new line. The text will be placed right after the prompt. You will also need to convert the string into a number for the program to work. You don't need to have a specific parameter for this either. If you do the following option with just the parentheses and nothing inside, you will get the same result and sometimes makes it easier.

Files

For the most part, you will use the print function to get a string to print to the screen. This is the default of the print function, but you can also use this same function as a good way to write something onto a file. A good example of this is

With open('myfile.txt', 'w') as myfile:

Print("Hello!",file=myfile)

Now this may look like a simple equation, but there is quite a bit that is going on in the string above that you should watch out for. In the spot *with* you opened up the myfile.txt to write on and then assigned it to the variable called myfile. Then in the second part, you wrote in Hello! To the file as a new line and then the *w* told the program that you will only be able to write the changes when the file is open.

Of course, you don't have to use the print function to get it to do the work that you want. The *write* method will often work well too. For example, you can replace the print with write like the example below to get the same things.

With open('myfile.txt', 'w') as myfile:

myfile.write("Hello!")

So far we have learned how to print a string of words into the program and even how to save them to a specific file. In addition to those options, you can use the read method in order to open a specific file and then to read the data that is there. If you would like to open and read a specific file, use this option:

***With** open('myfile.txt', 'r') **as** myfile:*

data = myfile.read()

with this option, you will be able to tell the program to read the files contents into variable data. This can make it easier to open up the programs that you would like to read.

Built In Types

Your computer is capable of processing a lot of information including numbers and characters. The types of information that the Python program will use are known as types and the language will contain many different types to help make things easier. Some of these include string, integers, and floating point numbers. Programmers can even define these different types using classes.

Types will consist of two separate parts. The first part is a domain that will contain a possible set of values and the second part is a set that contains the possible operations. Both of these can be performed on any value. An example of this is that if you have a domain that is a type of integer, it can only contain integers inside it including addition, division, multiplication, and subtraction.

One thing to note with this is that Python is a dynamically typed program. This means that there really isn't a need to specify the types for the variables when you create it. The same variables can be used to store the values of different types. Despite this, Python still needs you to have all the variables with a definitive type. For example, if the programmer tried to add in a number to a string, the Python program would recognize this and show an error. It won't try to figure out what you wanted; rather it will just exit without trying.

Integers

If you want to use integers as a type, you need to keep them as whole numbers. These can be positive or negative numbers, as long as there are no decimals with these numbers. If you have a decimal point in the number, even if the number is 1.0, you will need to use it as a floating point number instead. Python is able to display these integers in the "print" function, but only if it is the sole argument.

Print(3)

 # Let's add two numbers together

Print(1+2)

If you are using integers, you will not be able to place the two right next to each other. This is mainly because of how Python is a strongly typed language and won't recognize them if you combine them together. If you would like to put the number and the string together, you need to make sure that the number has turned into a string.

Operator Precedence

One thing that you need to keep track of when you are working in Python is operator precedence. For example, if you have 1+2//3 Python could interpret it as (1+2)//3 or 1+(2//3). Python has a method that will help you to order the operation properly so that you get the right information to come up. For example, when it comes to integer operation, Python is going to handle everything that is brackets first. Then it will handle the things that have**, then *, and then //, then %, +, and finally -.

If you are writing an expression that has a number of operations in it, you will need to keep those signs in mind. This will tell Python how to go through the numbers so that you can get the right answers at the time. Keep in mind that most arithmetic operators are going to be left associative so write it out that way for Python to read. The only exception is the ** feature. For example:

*# ** is right-associative*

2**3**4

 # will be evaluated right to left:

2**(3**4)

Strings

While a string may seem like something complicated, in Python they are basically a sequence of characters. They are going to work the same way as a list does, but they will contain a bit more functionality that is specific to the text.

Formatting strings can be a challenge when it comes to writing out your out your code. There are some messages that aren't going to be fixed string and sometimes there are values that are stored inside variables inside it. There is a way to get this to work right for string formatting. An example of this is:

Name = "Janet"

Age = 24

Print(*"Hello! My name is %s."* **%** *name)*

Print(*"Hello! My name is %s and I am %d years old."* **%** *(name, age))*

The symbols that have a % first are called placeholders. The variables that go into these positions will be placed after the % in the order where they are placed in the string. If you are doing just a single string, you will not need a wrapper, but if you do have more than one of these, you need to place them into a tuple, with a () enclosing it. The placeholder symbols will start with different letters, depending mostly on the variable type you are using. For example, the age is going to be an integer by the name is a string. All of these variables are going to be converted into the string before you can add them into the rest.

Escape Sequences

Escape sequences can be used as a way to denote special characters that can be hard to type on your keyboard. In addition, they can be used to denote characters that can be reserved for something else. For example, using and in the sequence can confuse the program so you may use the escape sequence to replace that like the following example:

Print("This is a line. \nThis is another line.")

Triple Quotes

We have spent a bit of time talking about both single and double quotes, but there are times when you may need to bring in the triple quote. This is used when you need to define a literal that will span many lines or one that already has a lot of quotes in it. To do this, just use a single and double together or three singles. The same rule applies with the triple quote as with all the others. You will need to star and end the phrase with the same one.

String Operations

One of the string operations that you may use a lot is a concatenation. This is used in order to join a pair of strings together and you will notice it is there with the + symbol. There are a lot of functions that Python is able to help you with and they will work with the strings to create a variety of operations. They are going to have some useful options that can do a lot more in the Pythons program

In Python program, strings are called immutable. This means that once you create the string, it is not capable of being changed. You may have to assign a new valuable to a specific variable that exists if you are looking to make some changes.

There is so much that you are able to learn about when it comes to getting started with Python. It may be a simple language, but you want to be able to learn how it works, how to write things down properly, and even how to leave a comment for others to understand when they are looking through the code. It may seem a bit intimidating in the beginning, but before too long, and with some practice, you will get it down and be writing your own code in no time.

Chapter 7: Variables and What They Do in Python

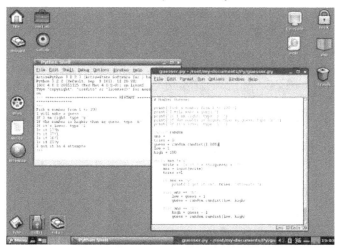

The next thing that we are going to discuss are variables. Variables are basically the labels that will denote where in your computers memory something is going to be stored and they can also hold values. When it comes to programming that is typed with statistics, the variables will each have a value that is predetermined and each variable is only going to hold the value of that type. Python has made it a bit easier because you can use one of your variables in order to store different types.

Think about your calculator for this one. The variable is going to be like the memory function in this calculator. It will hold onto a value so that you can retrieve it any time that you want, but when you store in a newer value, the older one will be erased. The only difference is that you will be able to have a large number of variables and each of them will have different values, each of them being referred by their own name.

With Python you will be able to define a variable by giving the label a value. For example, you can name a variable *count* and have it an integer value of one. You would show this by simply writing

count = 1

Note that with this syntax, you can assign a value to the variable with the same name. If you try to access values in a variable that hasn't been defined, the Python interpreter won't read through this. It will just exit out of the program and give you an error.

You can choose to define a few different variables in one line, but this is not the best practice for you to use. For example, you could do this:

 # Let's define three variables at the same time:
count, result, total = 0, 0, 0

And while that is the correct way to do things, it is much better to show it like this:

```
# This is the same as:

Count = 0

Result = 0

Total = 0
```

It is much easier to read the second way and will ensure that the Python program is going to understand what you want it to say.

Understanding the scope of a variable

You won't be able to access every variable from all parts of the program and not every variable will be the same length. The way that you defined the variable is going to determine where and how long you will be able to access this variable. The section of your program where you can access the variable is going to be known as the "scope" and the time that the variable will be available is known as the "lifetime".

Global variables are those that are defined within the main file body and you will be able to see these variables throughout the entire file as well as inside a file that will be able to import the specific file. These variables have far reaching effects and because of this, you may notice some consequences that you didn't notice. This is why most people won't use global variables, or they will use them sparingly. You should only add stuff into the global namespace if you plan to use them globally, like with functions or classes.

On the other hand, if you define a variable inside of another variable, it will be called a local variable. This one has the ability to be accessed from where it is defined and will only exist when that function executes. These are only going to be available in certain areas of the program and can't be found or used elsewhere.

The assignment operator

We have discussed this option a bit throughout the book, but haven't really given it a name. The assignment operator is the equals sign or the (=). It is going to be used in programming to assign the value to the right of the statement to the variable that is located t the left. Sometimes the variable will be created first. In cases where the value on the right is from an expression, such as an arithmetic expression, the evaluation will take place before this assignment happens.

Keep in mind that the (=) is not going to be a mathematical sign in programming. You can add things to the number and make all sorts of changes that wouldn't make sense if you thought of this sign as a mathematical one. Rather it is an assignment operator so that the statement will be turned into the part on the right.

When you assign the first value to this variable, you are going through the process of initializing. The definition of a value assignment and variable are carried out in the single step in this programming, although it is sometimes done in two steps with some of the other programming languages. But since it is done in one step, it is less likely that the user will make a mistake or receive an error in the process.

Modifying values

In some programming languages, you will be able to define a special variable that has a value that has been set. This means that the value can't be changed. These are called constants in the programming language. For the most part, Python is not going to allow for these kinds of restrictions, but there is a convention that is used to help ensure that some variables are marked to indicate that the values aren't supposed to be changed. To show this, the names will be written in CAPITAL letters with underscores between each word. An example of a variable that is a constants include:

NUMBER_OF_DAYS_IN_A_WEEK=7

NUMBER_OF_WEEKS_IN_A_YEAR=52

Of course, there are no rules to say you have to put the right number at the end. You could say there are 8 days in a week if you want because the Python program won't be keeping track, but it is best to just keep it accurate in case other coders would like to use it.

These can be really helpful to you in your string. Sometimes in the program, for example, you will want to change the maximum of a number that is allowed in the program. This may work fine for a bit, but maybe later on you need to increase or decrease this number. Without setting up a constants, you are going to have to go through and make quite a few changes to get everything matched up. But with a good constants in order, you can just go back to one place and get it all fixed up.

Understanding how the strings work in your program can make a big difference in the success that you see with this program. You need to learn where they are stored, what the rules are that govern each of them, and how to make them work in a specific part of the program. With a bit of practice, and using the guidelines above, you will get this down in no tie and can be an expert too!

Conclusion

Learning how to get started with computer programing can seem like a big challenge. There are many different programming options that you can go with, but many of them are hard to learn, will take some time to figure out, and won't always do all of the stuff that you need. Many people fear that they need to be really smart or have a lot of education and experience in coding before they are able to make it to the coding level they want. But with Python, even a beginner can get into programming.

Python has made it so easy to get started with coding whether you are a beginner or have been in this business for some time. The language is based in English so it is easy to read and it has gotten rid of a lot of the other symbols that make coding hard to read for others. And since it is user domain, anyone can make changes and see other codes to make things easier.

This guidebook has spent some time talking about the different functions that you can do in Python and how easy it is for a beginner to get started. You will find that this process is easy and you can learn it with a little bit of practice. It is easy to use, works across a lot of platforms, and even the newer Mac systems come with this already downloaded.

When you are ready to get started on programming, or you want to find a program that is going to do a lot of great things without all the hassle, make sure to check out Python. This is one of the most popular options when it comes to programming and you are going to find that it is easy to read and learn, even if you have no idea how to start in the first place. Use this guidebook to learn some of the basic functions and to learn a bit more about the Python program.

Python Programming for Intermediates
A Complete Crash Course on Python Programming

Adam Stewart

Table of Contents

Introduction

If you are looking for a great program that will allow you to write a great code without all the hassle or the messy code to read through, going with Python is one of the best options to choose. When you look at the code, you will see that it is really easy to read, even when you have no experience with writing code. When you get started with using it, you will see that it is really easy to understand and learn even though it still gives you the power that you are used to with some of the other language types.

For those who have had some experience with using programming languages, this is the guidebook for you. It is a comprehensive look at Python, providing some more examples and in-depth information on what you are able to do with the codes that you are learning. Not only are you going to get some information and a few syntaxes that you are going to have to figure out on your own, but you also get the chance to see some of these in work and learn how they will place on your computer when working in Python.

All of this will come together to give you some experience as well as the confidence that is needed to do really well with the Python language. While you may have some of the background information in programming or with Python in particular, getting started with this kind of code is sometimes scary and a bit confusion. But with the help of this guidebook, you are going to get some real life experience to work with and it will be easier than ever to get the work done for you.

So when you are ready to put some of your practical learning to use and you want to have some actual choices that will help you to see results when you want to put your codes to work, make sure to check out this guidebook and see how it can all work out for you without all the hassle or headaches.

Chapter 1: Getting Started with Python

Getting started with Python is a surprisingly easy process. You will love how simple this programming can be and how it will work on a lot of different programs. It is simple enough for the beginner to read through, once they learn some of the tricks of the trade, but it still has the power that you want when working on a programming language. It has the best of both worlds, which is why this programming language is one of the best options out on the market to choose from.

What is Python?

Python is a high level programming language that will use Object Oriented

Programming, or OOP. It is often used as a glue language to help connect other components together and can be used as a general purpose programming language. Because it is so versatile, it can be used with some of the more powerful programming languages, and easy to read, it gets rid of some of the brackets and other messy stuff that is in other languages, it has been ranked as one of the most popular languages for programming in the whole world.

If you are looking to create things like scripting interpreters, web applications, and even applications on the desktop, Python is the best program for you. It is considered open source right now, meaning that no one owns the rights to using it exclusively. This provides you with many different choices with the language as anyone can take the code and make it better all throughout the world. The best part is, it is powerful, can be placed on many different computers and computer systems, and it is free.

Versions of Python

There are a few different versions of Python that have come out over the years and they all have some different benefits as to why you should choose them. The most updated one is Python 3, although there are a few versions of this out right now. Most professionals are still using Python 2 because it is able to go back and work with older versions if needed while Python 3 is not able to do this. There are no newer versions of Python 2 that have come out in the past few years so it is likely that it is going to be phased out soon and Python users will have to stick with their older version or choose Python 3.

The original create of Python, Guido van Rossum choose to develop this language because it was simple, based on the English language, so that programmers new and old would be able to use the program without having too much complication. The language has undergone many changes throughout the years, especially since it has become open sourced for other companies and individuals to work with, but it has still maintained its simplicity and ability to work well with people who are new to programming.

Downloading Python

Let's have a little refresher course on how to download and install the Python program for those who may not have this program on their computers. You can download this program by visiting www.python.org/downloads or you can pick one of your favorite distribution sites and download the version that you want. You will need to select the python windows installer and then follow the simple steps that follow.

You should notice that the setup wizard will come up; it is easiest to just click on "Next" for all the options during the following steps in order to get everything to show up in default. If you would like to customize some things or make some changes, you are able to select these as well when going through the setup.

After Python has been successfully installed on the computer, you should select IDLE in order to get started. This is basically going to be the part that allows you to work on

Python so you need to make sure that you have it opened so that you can start writing your code. You will also need a text editor to work with so that the program is able to go through and read the work that you are doing. For a Windows computer, working with Notepad is a great option or you can pick out another option online.

How does Python Execute a Program

Each programming language that you work with is going to execute a program a bit differently. This is why it is so important to learn how to organize the words and the different statements that the program requires so that you avoid errors and other issues in your code. In this chapter, we will take some time to learn how Python will execute the commands that you give and basically how the whole program runs.

When you are working with Python, you are working with an interpreted programming language. You will have a text interpreter that will execute each of the programs going line by line and then will convert it into a code for the process to understand the words and carry them out for you.

Python is also a scripting language, so you can write out the script and then save it using the extension .py or you can directly write it and then execute each statement into the Python shell.

Internally, Python is going to work to compile your program, basically the source code, into a byte code that has the .pyc extension, just like the Java byte code. This makes it easier for the code to be executed without the delays and you will be able to see it come up in just a few seconds rather than waiting around.

You will be able to save your byte code files into a subdirectory that is called __pycache__ which is located in the directory where the source file resides. For example, if you wrote out helloworld.py it is going to then be converted into one of these byte codes and renamed helloworld.pyc.

You can go in and manually compile this code if something does go wrong, but for the most part, Python is going to do the compilation for you so it won't be an issues. As a beginner you may wonder where some of these .pyc suffixes come from, but Python is going to store them with that specific suffix so don't worry if it shows up.

Of course, this is only going to happen if Python has the write access, but even if the Python has no write access, it may not be saved that way, but the program is still going to work.

Whenever you call up a Python program, Python is going to check if there is already a compiled version with this .pyc suffix. This file should be newer than the .py suffix and if it exists, the Python will load in the byte code to speed up how fast the script is able to go. If the byte code doesn't exist on your computer, Python will work to create your byte code before it executes the program.

So basically, each time that you execute a script in Python, you will have a byte code created by the program as well. If the script in Python is imported like a module, your byte code is going to be stored in the proper .pyc file.

When you hear about implementation of Python, it means that the environment or the program that is providing support for executing your programs inside of the Python language, will be represented with the CPython reference implementation. This means that it is going to help you to work on executing the different codes and statements that you are working on within the program. There are also some variants of the CPython that you can work on and will make a big difference in the way that the program works. Some of the features that are available with the variants include:

- CrossTwine Linker—this is going to be a combination between CPython and an add-on library of your choice. It is going to offer some better performance when it comes to the code that you are working on.
- Stackless Python—this is CPython that has an emphasis on concurrency while using channels and tasklets. This is often the kind that is used for the dspython on programs like the Nintendo DS.
- Wypthon—this is considered a re-implementation of some of the parts of Python, which will drop the supports of using bytecode in order to use the wordcode

based omdel. It is going to use the stack register in the implementation and adds in lots of other types of optimization.

Implementation is everything when it comes to how you are able to work on your programs and can help you to get more done with Python compared to some of the other programming languages. What is so unique about Python is that it is able to work with a lot of other programming languages in order to still be simple to work on the code plus has all the power that you need to really get things done. Some of the other implementations that you may want to consider if you want to do something specific with the Python programming language include:

- Brython—this is one of the implementations that you can use in order to run Python in your browser using a translation to JavaScript so you can use these two together.
- CLPython—this is an implementation of Python in common lisp.
- HotPy—this is considered a virtual machine for Python that will support translation and bytecode optimization.
- IronPython—this is Python in C#. C# is a great programming language to use inside of the Windows platforms and is often a competitor to Python based on how popular and easy it is to use. This implementation allows you to translate your work from Python over to C# if you choose.
- Jython—this is the version of Python available for the Java platform.
- PyMite—this is Python that you can use for embedded devices
- PyPy—this is Python within Python so that you are able to target a few different environments at the same time.

- RapydScript—this is a language that is similar to Python that will compile into JavaScript so that you can use it in the Java platform without having to go with all of the difficult language issues.

Working on Python can be a great experience. If you are just a beginner with the idea of programming and are unsure about how to get all of this started, some of the other programming languages can be a bit confusing. Python is easy to use but has all the power that you want from some of the bigger names in programming language and you get the benefit of getting to use this program along with some of the other popular languages that you may want to work with!

Review of a Simple Program

As we mentioned, using Python is one of the simplest programming languages that you can choose. It isn't going to have a lot of excess around it like some of the other languages, which can save you a lot of time and effort.

It also makes it easier for you and for someone else to take a look at the information and be able to read through it. So let's take a look at some of the things that you can do with Python and how to get started with writing your first program.

The first program that we are going to write out is the "Hi World" program. This one is going to need a Python shell to make it easier and you will be able to test it out on your editors if you do it properly. This makes it easier to have a good idea of what you are doing and to catch any errors right in the beginning. If you are using the Python Shell, which works well on most of the computer types and programs that you may be using with Python, you will simply need to type in the following program to get the information to show up:

Print("Hi World!)

You should be able to go and execute this information and find that it will show up with the words Hi World! On the screen. This is a simple process to do, but it is going to help you to get things started and provides a good review of some of the simple steps that you need in order to start writing your own program on Python.

Remember that Python is a really easy programming language that won't have a lot of different brackets and other information that is in the way and will slow down what you are doing. It is also really easy to read.

As you can see, you only needed a few things in place in order to write out the phrase, rather than needing to type out lines of code to get the same result like you would need to do with other programming languages. Let's take a look at some of the other things that you are able to do with Python programming and how you can even write some good code to get your programs started.

Chapter 2: Some of the Basic Commands, Variables, Statements, and Other Things That You Can Do with Python

There are so many things that you are able to do in order to get a code up and running on Python. Many people may avoid using Python because they think that it is too simple or it just isn't going to get the job done. But in reality, it is simple just for the fact that even a beginner is able to learn how to use it, but that doesn't mean that you aren't able to do a lot with it. This chapter is going to take some time to look at the different commands that you can do with Python programming in order to make your programs and codes come to life.

Variables

Variables may sound like something that is too complicated to learn, but they are basically locations in the memory that are reserved in order to store the values of your code. When you work on creating a variable, you are reserving this spot in the memory. In some cases, the data type that is in the variable will tell the interpreter to save the memory space and can even decide what you are able to store on your reserved memory.

Assigning values to your variables

The value is going to be one of the basic things that your program will need to work with. it can be a string, such as Hi World, 3.14, which is considered a type float, or a whole number like 1, 2, 3 which is considered an integer. Python variables will not need an explicit declaration in order to reserve the space in the memory that you need. This is something that is going to happen automatically whenever you place a value with the variable. For this to work, simply place the (=) so that the value knows where it is supposed to go.

Some examples of this include:

X = 10   *#an integer assignment*

Pi = 3.14   *#a floating point assignment*

Y= 200   *#an integer assignment*

Empname = "Arun Baruah"   *#a string assignment*

Keep in mind that when you are working on codes, you are able to leave a comment with your wok by using the # sign. This allows you to explain what is going on in the code, leave some notes, or do something else within the program. It is not going to be read by the interpreter since it is just a little note that you are leaving behind for yourself or for someone else.

The next part is going to depend on which version of Python you are using. Python 2 is fine with you writing out print and then the information you want to talk about but Python 3 is going to require you to place the parenthesis in to make it work. An example would be:

Print("y = %d" %y)

Print("x = %d" %x)

Pring("Employee Name is %s" %empname)

These would then be put through the interpreter and the outputs that you would get should be

X = 10

Y = 200

Employee Name is Arun Baruah

Now go through and put in this information to your program and see what comes up. If you didn't get the right answers like listed above, you should go and check that the work is done. This is a simple way to show what you are able to do with Python and get the answers that you need.

Multiple Assignments

In addition to working with the single variables that were listed above, you will also be able to work on multiple assignments. This means that you are going to be able to assign one value to several different variables at the same time. To do this, you would just need to place the equal sign between all of them to keep things organized and to tell the computer that the value is going to be with all of the variables together. You can keep them separated out if that is easier for you, but using this method is going to help you to send everything to the same memory location on the computer and will give the code a clearer look on your screen.

A good example of how to give more than one variable the same value includes:

```
a = b = c = 1
```

This is telling the code that you want all of them to be tied with the value of 1 and that all of these variables should have the same value and that you want to assign them all to the same location within your memory.

Standard Data Types

Another thing that you are able to work on when doing Python is the various data types. These are going to be used in your code in order to define the operations that you can do on each data type as well as explain to others the storage method that will be used for this kind of data. Python has five data types that are considered standard including:

- Numbers
- Dictionary
- Tuple
- List
- String
- Numbers

Number data types are the ones that will store the numeric values. They are going to be created as objects once you assign a value to them. There are also four different types of numericals that Python will support including

- Complex (such as complex numbers)
- Float (floating point real values
- Long (long integers that can also be shown as hexadecimal and octal.)
- Int (signed integers)

One thing to note is that while Python will allow you to use the lowercase l when doing the long form of a number, it is best to go with an uppercase L whenever you are using the letter. This is going to help you avoid confusion in reading the program between the l and the 1 as they look really similar. Any time that Python is displaying a long integer that has the l in it, you will see the uppercase L.

Strings

Strings are identified in Python as a contiguous set of characters that will be shown by the use of quotations marks. Python is going to allow for either double quotes or single quotes, but you do need to keep things organized. This means that if you use a double quote at the beginning of your string, you need to end that same string with the double quote. The same goes when you are using a single quote. Both of these will mean the same thing, you just need to make sure that you are using the proper quote marks to make the code look good and to avoid confusing the Python program.

In addition to being able to print off the string that you would like, you are also able to tell the program to print just part of the string using some special characters. Let's look at some of the examples of what you are able to do with the strings, and the corresponding signs that you will use at well, to help illustrate this point.

str = 'Hi Python!'

print(str) #prints complete string

```
print(str[0])      #prints the first character of the string

print(str[2:5])   #prints characters starting from the 3rd to the 5th

print(str[2:])     #prints string starting from the 3rd character

print(str*2)       #prints the string two times

print(str+"Guys")    #prints concatenated string
```

For the most part you are probably going to want to print out the whole string to leave a message up on your program so the first print that you do is going to be enough. But if you just want to print out Hi or some other variation of the words above, you may find that the other options are really useful. You can do any combination of these, they are just examples to help you get started!

Lists

Lists are one of the most versatile data types that you can work on in Python. In this language, the list is going to contain different items that are either enclosed with the square brackets or separated out with commas.

They are similar to the arrays that you would see in C if you've worked with that program. The one difference that comes up with these is that the items that are in a list can be from different data types.

The values that are stored inside the list can be accessed with a slice operator as well as the [:} symbol with the indexes starting at 0 at the beginning of the list and then working down until you get to -1. The plus sign will be the concatenation operator while you can use the asterisk as the repetition operator. For some examples of what all this means and how you can use the different signs within your programming, consider some of these examples:

list = ['mainu', 'shainu', 86, 3.14, 50.2]

tinylist = [123, 'arun']

print)list)#prints complete list

print(list[0])   #prints the first element of the list

print(list[1:3]- #prints elements starting from the second element and going to the third

print(list [2:]) #prints all of the elements of the list starting with the 3rd element.

Print(tinylist*2)   #prints the list twice.

Print(list + tinylist)   #prints the concatenated lists.

Tuples

The next thing that we need to learn about for the Python language is about tuple. This one is pretty similar to what you are going to find with a list, but it is going to use some different signs. The main difference though is that lists will use brackets and the elements, as well as the size, can be changed through the program.

On the other hand, the tuples are going to use parentheses and you will not be able to update them. A good way to think about tuples is that they are going to be like a read only page.

As long as you don't try to make changes to the tuple in the program, you are going to be able to use it in the same way as you did the list examples above. This makes it a great option to use if you're looking for something that is simple but won't let anyone make changes to the program after you are done.

Dictionary

Dictionaries are another kind of tool that you can use when you are working in Python. They are similar to a hash table type and they are going to work similar to the hashes or the arrays that you can find on other programming languages like C# and Perl.

They will also consist of key value pairs and while the key can be almost any type on Python, you will notice that they are usually going to be strings or numbers. For the most part, when it comes to values, you will find that they are an arbitrary object in python.

Some examples of how this will work include the following codes:

```
#dictionary stores key-value pair, later to be retrieved by the values with the keys

dict = {}

dict['mainu'] = "This is mainu"

dict[10] = 'This is number 10"

empdict = {'name': 'arun', 'code':23, 'dept': 'IT'}


print(dict['mainu']) #this will print the value for the 'mainu' key

print(dict[10])          #this will print the value for the 10 key

print(empdict)           #this will print the complete dictionary

print(empdict.keys())  #this will print out all of the keys

print(empdict.values())      #this will print all the values
```

One thing to keep in mind is that these dictionary values are not going to be stored in an order that is sorted. They aren't going to have the concept of ordering among the elements. This does not mean that you can say that the elements are out of order, they are just going to be unordered.

Keywords

Most of the types of programming languages that you will deal with will have some keywords or words that are reserved as part of the language. These are words that you really shouldn't use in your code unless you absolutely can't help it.

There are 33 keywords found in the most recent version of Python and you will need to spell them properly if you want them to do the job that you lay out. The 33 keywords that you should watch out for include:

False

Class

Finally

Is

Return

None

Continue

For

Lambda

Try

True

Def

From

Nonlocal

While

And

Del

Global

Not

Yield

As

Elif

If

Or

Assert

Else

Import

Pass

Break

Except

In

Raise

Keep this list on hand if you are worried about learning the language. It will be able to help you out any time that you have issues with the interpreter about the names that you are giving the variable. You may be confused about why it is giving you some issues with the words you chose, you can go through with this list and see if you used one of the keywords inappropriately within your code.

When you are writing your code in the Python language, you are going to be making expressions and statements to get it done. Expressions are going to be able to process the objects and you will find them embedded within your statements.

A statement is basically a unit of code that will be sent to the interpreter so that it can be executed. There are two types of statements that you can use; assignment so far and print.

You will be able to write out the statement, or multiple statements, using the Python Shell to do so interactively or with the Python script using the .py extension that we talked about later.

When you type these statements into the interactive mode, the interpreter will work to execute it, as long as everything is properly in place, and then you can see the results displayed on the screen. When there are quite a few lines that you need to write in code, it is best to use a script that has a sequence of statements. A good example of this is:

```
#All of these are statements
X = 56
Name = "Mainu"
```

Z = float(X)

Print(X)

Print(Name)

Print(Z)

Operands and operators

There are a lot of great symbols that are going to show up when you make a code in your Python program. It is important to understand what parts you are able to work with and what they are all going to mean. Operators are often used to mean subtraction, addition, division, and multiplication. The values of the operator will be called operands. You can use many different signs for these in order to get the values that you would like to see.

While you are using the operators and operands, you need to remember that there is going to be an order of evaluation that is followed. Think about going back to math class and how this all worked. You had to look for specific signs in order to figure out which tool you were supposed to use in order to come up with the right answer. This is the same when using these operands within your code.

When you have more than one of these operators in the expression, you will need to do the order of evaluation based on the rules of precedence. For anything that is arithmetic, Python is going to use the acronym PEMDAS which is parenthesis, exponentiation, multiplication, division, addition, and subtraction. If there are a number of these that are the same, such as two sets of numbers that need to be multiplied together, you will need to work from left to right to get the correct number.

Another important operator that you should look for is the modulus operator. This one is going to work with integers and is going to yield the remainder once the first operand has been divided by the second one.

. for Python

One thing that you will find useful with Python is that you are able to send out . in the program. This allows you to add in something to explain what you are working on rather than just leaving it up to the other programmer to figure out. You will simply need to bring in the # sign in order to denote that you are going to leave a little bit of a comment or statement about the code.

Any time that you use the # symbol, the program interpreter is going to ignore what you say rather than trying to write it. While the computer program is ignoring it, it is still there for the programmer to look at if needed.

Using the Python language does not need to be difficult, but you do need to be able to understand what is going on in each part and how all of them are going to help you to get the results that you need. Each one will work slightly differently so that you are able to get the right codes done in Python.

Chapter 3: Understanding the Decision Control Structure

There are times in life that you are going to have to make decisions based on the situation around you. Perhaps you woke up one morning and wanted to go for a walk, but it started to rain out. Did you just sit there blankly without another option to help you out? No, you may have woken up and decided to grab an umbrella and go on the walk anyway or you may decide to stay home and read a book. You can make other decisions, even if the first one doesn't work out, based on the circumstances around you.

Now this is kind of the same idea when it comes to working with Python. So far we have just told the program to do one thing at a time. If the circumstances don't line up exactly with the program, you are not going to get any results. This just won't work for some programs, especially if the other people are allowed to pick from a couple of different answers. The decision control structure is the part that allows you to pick a couple different options for Python in case the first choice doesn't work out.

For the most part, these are going to work on a true of false kind of outcome. You will need to figure out which action you want to take and what statements the program should execute if the outcome is either true or false. In Python, any answer that is non-null or non-zero is going to be considered true and the ones that are either null or zero will be considered false. To understand some of these consider the following:

- If statements—the if statement is going to consist of a Boolean expression that is then followed by one or more statements that will be executed if the answer matches up.
- If...else statements—this option will have a statement that will show up if the "if" statement is correct, but there is also another statement that is told to com if the Boolean expression ends up being false.
- Nested if statements—you can use one if or if else statement inside another when needed.

Some examples of how this works includes:

age = 23

if (age == 23):

    print("The age is 23")

print("Have a good day!")

when this code comes through it is going to state:

The age is 23

Have a good day!

'ing the "if" keyword is going to tell the compiler that what you are writing is a

'ion control instruction. The condition that is behind the keyword if it is inside the

eses. The conditions will need to be true if you want the code to come out, but if

ie, this statement is just going to be ignored in this situation and it is going to

he next command that you give.

ie up

you could set up an "if…else" clause. This one would show the

one

he conditions were true. But, if the conditions ended up being false,

ng out a second statement instead. This can help to ensure that you

ssage across no matter what someone else is sending over and

om completely ignoring this step.

s

ay be asking is how we are able to tell whether the
th

ill need to use some of the relational operators to make
eq

e able to compare the two values to see if they are

me of the options that you can use to see if a

statement is right include:

This expression	Is true if
X == y	X is equal to y
X != y	X is not equal to y
X < y	X is less than y
X > y	X is greater than y
X <= y	X is less than or equal to y
X >= y	X is greater than or equal to y

A good example of this would be:

age = int(input("Enter your age:"))

if (age <=18):

   print("You are not eligible for voting, try next election!")

print("Program ends")

This code will print you out a different example based of the age that is put in. Since it is an if statement only, you are going to get an answer just when the number is 18 or under. Here we will look at the output based on the age of 18 and that of 35.

Enter your age :18

You are not eligible for voting, try next election!

Program ends

Enter your age :35

Program ends

Now we should take a look at adding in multiple statements within your "if" statement. It is not uncommon to find two or more statements being placed inside an expression and working just fine if everything is satisfied. If these statements are executed, you will need to make sure that you indent them properly. Let's take a look at how this could work. Make sure to give this a try on your interpreter to get some experience with typing code and how the "if" statements are going to work.

bonus = 0.0

currentyear = int(input("Enter current year:"))

yearofjoining = int(input("Enter year of joining:"))

yearofservice = currentyear – yearofjoining

if(yearofservice >2):

    bonus = 1500

    print("Bonus - %d" %bonus)

    print("Congratulations! We are able to provide you a bonus o %d" %bonus).

Now if the "if" statement does end up being higher than two, you will find that the congratulations statement is going to come out. But if the amount is lower than two, you are going to end up with no statements because all of the statements were not met. You can place whatever numbers that you want inside it in order to get it to work for each employee in this option.

The "if-else" Statement

So far we have just been talking about the "if" statements. These are ones that need to be true before you are able to see any of your statements come out. If things come out to be false, there will be no statement at all. Now this does work at times, but in other instances, you may want to have a few different statements come up.

With the "if else" statement, you can pick two, and sometimes more, statements that are going to come up based on the results. If your results end up being true, you will have the first statement come up, but if the results end up being false, you can pick another statement that you would like to show up as well. This ensures that you are getting an answer no matter the result so that the program shows something new.

You just need to make sure that after writing out your "if" statement, you add in the "else" and then put in the statements that you would like to have come up. This can take a bit of time to work, but it opens up so many great options with your code to make sure that it all evens out and looks nice with your code.

Another option that you can do with your statements is the elif statement. This one is going to give you the option of checking out a few expressions as true, rather than just one expression as true, so that you can execute the whole block of code once just one of the conditions turns up to be true. Of course, doing this is optional, but there is the benefit of being able to have any number of elif statements after the if.

Let's take a look at what all of this is going to look like in when you write it out in the syntax:

if expression1:

statement(s)

elif expression2:

statement(s)

elif expression3:

statement(s)

else:

statement(s)

You will then be able to place your information into the parts and get the answer that is listed with each of the parts. Let's take a look at this syntax expanded out a bit so that you are able to get an idea of how this works:

```
Print("Let's enjoy a Pizza! Ok, let's go inside Pizzahut!")
print("Waiter, Please select Pizza of your choice from the menu")
pizzachoice = int(input("Please enter your choice of Pizza: "))
if pizzachoice == 1:
        print('I want to enjoy a pizza napoletana')
elif pizzachoice == 2:
        print('I want to enjoy a pizza rustica')
elif pizzachoice == 3:
        print('I want to enjoy a pizza capricciosa')
else:
        print("Sorry, I do not want any of the listed pizza's, please bring a Coca Cola
for me.")
```

you will see the information that is listed after print show up for the first three lines. After the third line, the program should ask you to put in one of four options. Depending on which option you choose, you will be able to see the right answer, either the pizza of your choice or the option to just get a drink. It may look like a bit of a mess at first, but it helps you to get options that the code will be able to understand while returning the right "pizza type" to you in the process.

The "if" statements are going to provide you with a lot of help when you are looking to make some great things happen in your code. You can also use nested if statements that allow you to add a few of these within each other, adding some more power to your code. Of course, it may take some experience to get this all down, but you are going to be amazed at all that you are able to do when you are working on your codes.

Chapter 4: Loop Control Statements

So far, we have discussed a lot of programs and what you are able to do when you are working in Python, but these are all going to be either decision or sequential control instruction. For the first ones, we were doing calculations that will be carried out in a fixed order while with the second one, the right set of instructions were executed based on the outcome of the conditions that were tested.

There were some limitations just because of the way they are executed and they are only able to perform the exact same series of actions, always in the same way, and they are only able to do it one time.

There are times when you will want to write out a code that can be a bit more complicated. One of these options is for the loop statement. This kind of statement will allow the programmer to execute a statement, or even a group of statements, several times. If you have a statement that you would like to keep coming back in the program, you will want to create your own loop statement to make this happen.

It is possible to use Python in order to hand these loop statements and there are three methods that you can choose in order to make the loop statement happen. These three methods include:

- Nesting loops
- Using a for loop
- Using a while loop

Let's take some time to discuss all of these and figure out when and why you would use each of the methods when creating your new code.

The While Loop

The first type of loop that we will look at is the while loop. This is a good one when you want the code to do something for a fixed number of times. You don't want to have it go on indefinitely, but you do want to have it go for a certain amount of times, such as ten times, before stopping. Let's take a look at a good example of calculation of interest in the following example to help show how this works.

#calculation of simple interest. Ask user to input principal, rate of interest, number of years.

counter = 1

while(counter <= 3):

    principal = int(input("Enter the principal amount:"))

    numberofyeras = int(input("Enter the number of years:"))

    rateofinterest = float(input("Enter the rate of interest:"))

    *simpleinterest = principal * numberofyears * rateofinterest/100*

    print("Simple interest = %.2f" %simpleinterest)

    #increase the counter by 1

    counter = counter + 1

    print("You have calculated simple interest for 3 time!")

The output is going to come out to allow the user to put in the information that they want to compute. It will figure out the interest rates and the amount that is going to be calculated based on the numbers that you provide. It will go on a loop so that they are able to do this three times for use of this. You can set it up to take on more if you would like, but for this one we are just using it three times for simplicity.

This is for loops that you will use when you want a piece of code to repeat a certain amount of times. It is a bit different than the one above because it is more of the traditional way to do things, but it can still be useful. This option is going to be a bit different than what you will find in C++ and C.

Rather than this loop giving the user the chance to define the halting condition or the iteration step, Python is going to have the statement iterate over the items in the order that they show up within the statement. An example of this is below:

Measure some strings:

words = ['apple', 'mango', 'banana', 'orange']

for w in words:

print(w, len(w))

When it goes through the loop with this, you are going to get the four fruit words above come out in the order that they are written. If you want them to be done in a different order, you will need to place them in a different order when you are putting them into the syntax in order to avoid confusion. You will not be able to make changes to the words once they are already in the syntax like above.

If for some reason you want to iterate just over a specific sequence of numbers, using the function range() can really come in handy with this. It is going to generate a whole list containing some of the arithmetic progressions that you are looking to use.

It is also possible to do a nested loop. This is basically just one loop that is inside of another one and it will keep going until both of the programs are done. This can be useful for a number of things that you want to do with your program, but we will show an example that will give out the multiplication table going from 1 to 10:

#write a multiplication table from 1 to 10

For x in xrange(1, 11):

For y in xrange(1, 11):

*Print '%d = %d' % (x, y, x*x)*

When you got the output of this program, it is going to look similar to this:

1*1 = 1

1*2 = 2

1*3 = 3

1*4 = 4

All the way up to 1*10 = 2

Then it would move on to do the table by twos such as this:

2*1 = 2

2*2 = 4

And so on until you end up with 10*10 = 100 as your final spot in the sequence.

These loops can help you to get a number of things to show up on your computer, sometimes indefinitely, but for the most part they are going to keep going through the loop only for the amounts of times that you would like it to. You will be able to put these loops in with a bit of practice and there are so many things that you can do.

For example, the simple formula above will give you the whole multiplication table started with 1*1 and ending with 10*10. For such a simple statement, you are getting a great amount of information from it and many of the loops that you work with will be the same.

Chapter 5: Functions

Functions are another important part of learning the Python language. These are basically blocks of code that are self-contained and will be able to perform some kind of coherent task within your code. When you take the time to define a function, you will be able to specific the name of the function as well as the sequence of the statements. You will then be able to call up the function using its name. There are two types of functions that we are going to use here and we will discuss them below.

User defined functions

With this one, you will be able to define the functions that you are using. They are going to have pretty much the same rules that you found with variable names. This means that using underscore characters, numbers, and letters will work great, but you should never use a number for the first character in the function. You can't use your keywords as the name of your function and you should be careful about having a function and a variable that have the same name.

The empty parentheses that you will see after the name will show that the function isn't going to take on any arguments. The first line is going to be known as the header while the rest of the function is known as the body. You need to make sure that the header ends with a colon and that you indent in the body so that the interpreter knows what you are doing. A good example of the syntax or a function includes:

def functionname(arg1, arg2, arg3):

 '"docstring of the function i.e., a brief introduction about the function"

 #code inside the function

 Return[value]

 #a function may not have any arguments or parameters like

 def functionname():

 #code inside the function

Using the parameters of a function can be valid in any of the data types that you are using with Python, whether you are dealing with user-defined classes, dictionary, tuple, list, float, and int. Let's take a look at some of the different parts of this function so you can understand the importance of each one and how they work.

Docstring function

Now let's take a look at the docstring. The first string that you see right after the header in a function is going to be called the docstring, something that is short for documentation string. It is going to be used in the code in order to explain what the function does. This is an optional part, but it is a good practice to get into. If you are planning on having this go across a few lines, you should consider doing the triple quotes in order to tell the computer what you are doing.

The return statement

The function is always going to give back a value. The return statement is going to be used as an exit function and will go back to the place where it was called from. This statement is allowed to contain expressions that it can evaluate before giving out a value. If there are no expressions within the statement, or the return statement is not even present inside of the function, you will find that the return you get is the None object.

Lifetime and scope variables

Another thing that you can learn about the Python language is about lifetime and scope variables. The scope variable is the part that is going to be recognized and visible. The variables and the parameters that are inside the function are not going to be visible from the outside eye (those who are looking at the code when it is being executed) but they will have a local scope that can show up.

On the other hand, a lifetime is the period of time that the variable is going to exist in the memory. The lifetime of most variables inside functions will be as long as your function executes. After the function returns the value, these are going to be destroyed so that you can put in no inputs and get different results. For example, if you input certain numbers and your return ends up being 5, the next time you are able to put in different information and you may get a 6. These will delete after each function has run through so that you can get new results if new information is put inside.

Pass by references

In Python, all of the parameters that you put in are going to be passed by reference. This means that the address of the location in the memory is going to be referenced to the memory location. So if you are going to change what your parameter is able to refer to inside the function, this same change is then going to reflect back when you are doing the calling function.

Flow of execution

The execution of the statement is always going to start right at the first statement that is inside of the programs. Your statements are going to be done just one at a time to avoid confusion and make sure that the program is running as smoothly as it should. The execution is also going to happen going from top to bottom so you need to make sure that you are putting them in properly. So you must make sure that you are defining the functions before you decide to call them up to get the right order.

Anonymous functions

Python allows the programmer to create anonymous functions. These are functions that are not going to be bound to a name at run time and you are going to need to use a construct that is known as "lambda." This operator is a way to create these functions that don't have a name. basically you will want to create these when the functions are considered throw away, or they are just needed right where they have been created. There are a few functions that Lambda functions will work with including reduce(), map(), and filter().

The syntax that you will want to use with the lambda function is:

lambda argument_list: expression.

The reduce, filter, and map function

We have talked about a number of functions so far in this book, but it time to look at a few that are going to help you to get more out of the code that you are writing. Particularly, we are going to take a look at the map, filter, and reduce functions, as well as list comprehension to help you get started.

Map function

The map() function is the one that will apply to ever member inside of an iterable, or those inside a list. For the most part, you would use the anonymous inline function to make this work, though this is one o them that you are able to use inside of any of your functions. So i you are trying to work on a list, this would be a good one for you to use in your computer code.

Filter function

Next on the list is the filter function. Just like you would guess from the name, the filter is able to extract the elements in the sequence for which the function returns a true. The rest would be ignored. This means that you will want to do a sequence that would be either true or false in order to get this one to work. When the sequence has a few options that are true, the filter function will pick out those ones. On the other hand, if all of them, or at least some of the sequence points, are false, you will find that these are not filtered out.

The reduce function

This one is a bit unique. It is going to take several values to the sequence and will work it until you end up with just one value, rather than the large list that you have. It is going to work from let to right in order to get the answers that you are looking for. Depending on the length of your sequence, you may have to do some work with this to get it all done.

Let's look at the numbers 1, 2, 3, and 4. The reduce function is going to take these four numbers and turn them into one. It will do this by adding the 1 and the 2 together to get 3, then adding the 3 and the 3 together to get six, and then adding the 6 and the 4 together to get 10. In this answer you will get the single value of 10.

A good syntax to show how this works is

from functools import reduce

results = reduce((lambda x, y: x +y), [1, 2, 3, 4])

print(result)

List comprehension

This is a great way to create some lists inside of Python. Some of the common applications will use your elements to make the new list and others will create a subsequence of these elements when they satisfy certain conditions. The list comprehension feature can actually be a substitute to using the lambda function as well as the other functions that we just talked about. This is because the list function is easier to work with and understand. The syntax of using the list comprehension is

*[expression-involving-loop-variable **for** loop-variable **in** sequence]*

This is going to step right over all the elements of the sequence so that you are able to set up the loop variable for ever element one at a time and then it completely eliminates what you needed the lambda function for in the first place.

www.ingramcontent.com/pod-product-compliance
Lightning Source LLC
LaVergne TN
LVHW051708050326
832903LV00032B/4068